A Student Review Book for AP United States History

by

Michael Henry, Ph.D.

DORRANCE PUBLISHING CO., INC.
PITTSBURGH, PENNSYLVANIA 15222

All Rights Reserved
Copyright © 1997 by Michael Henry, Ph.D.
No part of this book may be reproduced or transmitted
in any form or by any means, electronic or mechanical,
including photocopying, recording, or by any information
storage or retrieval system without permission in
writing from the publisher.

ISBN # 0-8059-4093-6
Printed in the United States of America

First Printing

For information or to order additional books, please write:
Dorrance Publishing Co., Inc.
643 Smithfield Street
Pittsburgh, Pennsylvania 15222
U.S.A.

Dedication

To my wife, Ann, and my daughter, Kimberly.

Contents

Introduction vii
Research: What Type of Questions Appear on the Test 1
Review Lessons:
1. Famous Rebellions in United States History 6
2. Presidents of the United States 1789-1974 8
   Great Presidents of the United States 11
3. Historical Periods 12
4. Coming of the American Revolution 14
5. The National Banks, 1791 and 1816 16
6. Liberal Versus Conservative in United States History 18
7. Political Parties in the Nineteenth Century 20
8. Freedom of the Seas and Wars with Europe 23
9. Compromises and the Union 25
10. The Marshall Court and the National Period 27
11. Cornerstones of United States Foreign Policy 29
12. Expansion of the United States 1783-1853 31
13. Wars in United States History 34
14. Amendments to the Constitution 37
15. The Abolitionist Movement 39
16. Women's Movement in the Nineteenth Century 41
17. Major Treaties in United States History 43
18. Reconstruction of the South 45
19. The Judicial Road to *Plessy* 47
20. Black Leaders 1880-1968 49
21. Reform Movements of the Twentieth Century 51
22. The Three R's of the New Deal 53
23. American Involvement in Vietnam 55
24. Containment 1945-1975 57
25. Famous Doctrines: From Monroe to Nixon 60

Introduction

I am a long-time teacher and student of the Advanced Placement United States history program. I have taught AP United States history since 1977, graded the essay portion of the test for eight years, and given workshops on AP United States history in the mid-Atlantic region for many years. In addition I wrote my doctoral dissertation on the AP United States history program and have published five articles on the test. I offer this resume not as self-promotion, but rather to support the contents of this book as the product of many years of experience and scholarship with the AP United States history curriculum.

This book is designed to assist you in preparing for the AP United States history examination. Although many of the activities can be presented during the academic year, they are probably best used in the six weeks prior to the test.

The materials are based on a fundamental principle: There is no magic bullet or quick, easy road to success on the AP history examination. Nothing can replace competent classroom instruction and dedicated study. It is only through your daily efforts in building historical knowledge and writing skills that you are likely to qualify for college credit on the AP history test. If you have not read the assigned readings, completed your homework, and taken notes in class, these review ideas are unlikely to enable you to master the AP examination.

Yet, the materials that follow can help you organize your review program as you tackle the daunting task of preparing for a test covering a full year of academic work. The book targets some critical areas of the United States history curriculum. It offers significant information about important topics, and it can guide you in preparing your own review outlines and charts. It is my hope that these review materials can be models to follow as you build your own review program. Again ultimately success on the test is your responsibility.

I have prefaced each review item with some historical background to the topic and suggested ways to use it. You may find other uses of the materials as well. The main point is that you see these materials as a supplement to the work you and your teacher have done during the academic year.

In closing I once again emphasize that none of what follows can replace your comprehensive, college-level survey of United States history from 1607-1970. These materials can be an important addendum to improving performance, but in the final analysis, success on the AP history test can only come from your day-to-day efforts in class.

What Types of Questions Appear on the Test

I analyzed both the essay portion and the multiple-choice section of the test over time. I was interested in what types of questions appeared on the test. The essay part of the test consists of two parts—a document-based question (DBQ) and two free-response essays. The DBQ requires student to analyze and use primary sources as they formulate an answer. With the free-response section, students are given some choice and asked to demonstrate written mastery of historical events.

In my research on the free-response essay section[1], I traced the trends in the essay from 1963 to 1992 by developing a categorization system that produced a matrix of essay questions in five-year periods for those thirty years (Table 1). The seven categories of questions were:

1. *Intellectual and cultural issues*: Questions addressing how literature, art architecture, and religion influenced United States history.

2. *Minority issues*: Questions addressing the role of African-Americans, women, and Native Americans in the development of the United States.

3. *Political issues*: Questions addressing evolution of political parties, legislative action, Supreme Court rulings, presidential administrations, and reform movements.

4. *Military and diplomatic issues*: Questions addressing American involvement in armed conflicts and relations with other nations.

5. *Historiographic issues*: Questions addressing the history of history, as well as schools of historical interpretation.

---

[1] Michael S. Henry, "The AP United States History Examination: Have Free Response Essays Changed in the Last Thirty Years?" *Social Education* (March 1994): 145-148.

6. *Economic and business issues*: Questions addressing employment, monetary policy, labor relations, and industrial and agricultural developments.
7. *Immigration issues*: Questions addressing trends in immigrations and how immigration influenced American development.

As indicated in Table 1, political, military, and diplomatic questions dominated the essay section in the three decades of analysis (55.3 percent). Economic questions were also very likely to appear on the examination (19 percent), with some attention given to intellectual and minority issues (10.2 percent). The least numerous essay questions on the test were historiography (2.8 percent) and immigration (2.3 percent).

I also analyzed the multiple choice section[2]. This part of the examination now consists of eighty questions, which carries 50 percent of the test credit. Approximately 16 percent of the questions come from the period through 1789, 50 percent deal with the years 1790-1914, and 33 percent come from 1915 to the present. Based on the two most recently published tests (1984, 1988), about 5-8 percent of the questions come from the period 1955 to the present.

In the mid 1980s, Educational Testing Service allowed me to examine the multiple choice section of the test from 1960-1984. For purposes of analysis, I arranged the 2,035 items into six categories:

1. *Primary document questions*: Concerned reading passages from original sources such as diaries, state and national laws, executive agreements, and government documents.
2. *Historigraphic questions*: Concerned the history of history, as well as schools of historical interpretation.
3. *Symbolic representation questions*: Concerned the interpretation of cartoons, graphs, and maps.
4. *Arts and humanities questions*: Concerned American literature, architecture, painting, and sculpturing.
5. *Social Science questions*: Concerned concepts, facts, and skills from economics, sociology, and anthropology. Questions addressed employment, monetary policy, and labor relations. Further they concerned the roles of African-Americans, women, and Native Americans in the development of the United States.

---

[2] Michael S. Henry, "The Advanced Placement American History Examination: How Has It Changed?" *The Social Studies* (July/August 1987): 159-162.

6. *Traditional questions*: Concerned the evolution of political parties, legislation, Supreme Court rulings, presidential administrations, and reform movements. In addition they dealt with American involvement in armed conflicts and relations with other nations.

The categorization of the multi-choice questions produced a matrix presented in Table 2. As with the findings on the essay portion of the examination, the multiple-choice section featured many traditional questions (36 percent). While primary documents appeared to play a significant role on the test, they showed a steady decline in the thirty years of investigation. They fell from a high of almost 40 percent in the 1960s to only 13 percent in the 1980s. Much of the decline is attributable to the introduction of the DBQ in 1973.

Also, like the essay section, the multiple-choice portion of the test had many social science questions (20.8 percent). The least numerous types of questions came from historiography (2.1 percent) and the arts (4.6 percent).

Several conclusions are apparent from this analysis of the AP test:

1. Questions about politics, military events, and diplomacy predominated on the examination. Instructionally these areas should form the core of the survey course.
2. Questions about economics, business, minorities, and women are also very important on the test. These areas should also be emphasized during the year.
3. Historiography is not emphasized on the test.
4. Questions on the arts and immigration are not numerous on the AP history test, and in the crowded curriculum, they may play a marginal role in classroom instruction.
5. Primary documents play an important role on the test as part of the DBQ process. All classes should make analysis and synthesis of primary documents a major component of instruction to ready students for this required essay.

The review materials that follow coincide with these trends. They emphasize politics, diplomacy, economics, civil rights, and military events. These materials are keyed to areas that are likely to appear on the test and are likely to help your preparation for it.

Table 1
Free Response Essays by Five-year Periods
1963-1992

Years	Intell. Cultural	Minority	Political	Military Diplomat	Histori- ography	Econ. Business	Imm. grat.	Totals
1963-67	4 (7.6%)	1 (1.9)	20 (37.7)	11 (20.7)	3 (5.7)	11 (20.7)	3 (5.7)	53
1968-72	5 (10.0)	6 (12.0)	18 (36.0)	8 (16.0)	3 (6.0)	10 (20.0)	0 (0.0)	50
1973-77	5 (13.5)	6 (16.2)	14 (37.8)	5 (13.5)	0 (0.0)	6 (16.3)	1 (2.7)	37
1978-82	2 (8.0)	2 (8.0)	11 (44.0)	5 (20.0)	0 (0.0)	5 (20.0)	0 (0.0)	25
1983-87	5 (20.0)	4 (16.0)	7 (28.0)	4 (16.0)	0 (0.0)	4 (16.0)	1 (4.0)	25
1988-92	1 (4.0)	3 (12.0)	11 (44.0)	5 (20.0)	0 (0.0)	5 (20.0)	0 (0.0)	25
TOTAL	22 (10.2)	22 (10.2)	81 (37.6)	38 (17.7)	6 (2.8)	41 (19.0)	5 (2.3)	215

Table 2
Multi-choice Questions by Five-year Periods
1960-1984

Years	Total # of Questions	Primary Document	Histor- iography	Social Science	Arts and Humanities	Symbolic Repres.	Traditional
1960-64	300	118 (39.2%)	2 (1.0)	43 (14.2)	4 (1.3)	37 (12.3)	96 (32.0)
1965-69	375	130 (34.6)	1 (0.5)	62 (16.5)	10 (2.6)	55 (14.6)	117 (31.2)
1970-74	375	107 (28.6)	17 (4.5)	59 (15.8)	14 (3.7)	53 (14.1)	125 (33.3)
1975-79	485	108 (22.3)	15 (3.1)	121 (24.9)	25 (5.2)	32 (6.6)	184 (37.9)
1980-84	500	65 (13.0)	8 (1.6)	137 (27.4)	39 (7.8)	39 (7.8)	212 (42.4)
TOTAL	2035	528 (25.9)	43 (2.1)	422 (20.8)	92 (4.6)	216 (10.6)	734 (36.0)

Famous Rebellions

Rebellions helped shape American development before the Civil War. Three early uprising (Bacon's, Shays', and the Whiskey Rebellion) focused on economic and political grievances against a perceived arbitrary and distant authority. The following chart will help you analyze these rebellions.

As you consider the chart, you may wish to evaluate whether these early dissenters were driven by a rebellious nature, the frontier environment, unfair governmental action, or reacted to all these factors.

Nat Turner's revolt was a different type of rebellion. It was the great nightmare of the ante-bellum slavocracy—a large-scale slave revolt. Yet it stands alone as the only uprising of this type before the Civil War. Historians have speculated about why there were no other large-scale risings. How would you explain this lack of large-scale slave resistance?

Famous Rebellions

	Date	Cause	Event	Significance
Nathaniel Bacon's Rebellion	1676	• Frontiersmen/Indians clashed. • Frontiersmen demanded help. • Jamestown refused, feared Indian War.	• Bacon/Men stormed Jamestown. • Bacon died of fever. • Rebellion collapsed.	• Colonial rebellion against British authority. • Clash between: East/West; Rich/Poor. • Tidewater's discrimination against frontiersmen.
Daniel Shays' Rebellion	1786-1787	• Unfair taxes in Massachusetts. • Farms foreclosed.	• Shays/1200 men closed courts in western Massachusetts. • State militia put it down.	• General threat to property. • Articles of Confederation unable to maintain law and order. • Bolstered call for revisions of AOC. (Constitutional Convention 1787.)
Whiskey Rebellion	1794-1795	• Farmers in western Pennsylvania refused to pay taxes. • Attacked tax men. • Farmers compared tax to Stamp Act of 1765.	• Washington called for 13,000 men to suppress the rebels. • Rebels surrendered.	• Constitution more than paper. • Government would enforce the law. • Hamilton's idea of energetic government prevailed.
Nat Turner's Rebellion	1831	• Slaves wanted freedom. • Nat saw "vision," struck for freedom.	• Turner/100 slaves killed 57 whites. • Turner caught; executed with 100 other slaves.	• Frightened South. • Tightened Slave Codes. • Restricted freedom for all blacks in South.

Presidents of the United States
1789-1974

Most classes in United States history are taught chronologically. More specifically they are organized by presidential administrations. Your teacher probably presented the events of American history by associating when they happened with the occupants of the White House. The following two charts are designed to help re-create the presidential chronology you learned this year and to examine the four men who excelled as president.

The first chart is a summary of the presidents from George Washington to Richard Nixon. It includes their term of office, their party, and at least one event that occurred while they were in office. At this time of the year, you may be fuzzy about the order of the presidents and about distinctive events associated with some of our least-remembered presidents.

You should not attempt to memorize the chart; that would be confusing and counterproductive. You may, however, wish to study it so that you can link events like wars, depressions, and land acquisitions with various presidents. As you study the chart, you should also consider why there were groups of undistinguished presidents. The two eras of forgotten presidents were 1836-1860 and 1876-1901. Why do you think these two periods were characterized by presidential mediocrity?

The other chart summarizes the achievements of our four greatest presidents. In all cases, these leaders had major domestic successes and promoted America's strength and security in foreign relations. In addition each man changed American political thinking and transformed the presidency. Historians suggest that in order to achieve presidential greatness, a person must make the office "a more splendid instrument of democracy." What do you think this means? Do you feel any other presidents deserve the greatness label? Why?

United States Presidents

President	Term	Party	Major Event\Dev
1. George Washington	1788-1796	Fed.	Begins Government; Whiskey Rebellion; Farewell Address.
2. John Adams	1796-1800	Fed.	Undeclared War with France; Sedition Act.
3. Thomas Jefferson	1800-1808	Rep.	1st Republican; Louisiana Purchase, Embargo Act.
4. James Madison	1808-1816	Rep.	War 1812.
5. James Monroe	1816-1824	Rep.	Florida Purchase; Era of Good Feeling; Missouri Compromise.
6. John Q. Adams	1824-1828	Rep.	Corrupt Bargain.
7. Andrew Jackson	1828-1836	Demo.	Bank Battle; Tariff\Nullification; Indian Removal.
8. Martin Van Buren	1836-1840	Demo.	Panic 1837; Trail of Tears.
9. William Harrison	1840-1841	Whig	Died; First Whig.
10. John Tyler	1841-1844	Whig	Annexation of Texas.
11. James Polk	1844-1848	Demo.	Mexican-American War.
12. Zachary Taylor	1848-1850	Whig	Last Whig; Died.
13. Millard Fillmore	1850-1852	Whig	Compromise 1850.
14. Franklin Pierce	1852-1856	Demo.	Kansas\Nebraska Act.
15. James Buchanan	1856-1860	Demo.	Dred Scott Case; Seven States leave Union.
16. Abraham Lincoln	1860-1865	Rep.	Civil War; First killed.
17. Andrew Johnson	1865-1868	Union	Impeached
18. Ulysses S. Grant	1868-1876	Rep.	Reconstruction; many scandals.
19. Rutherford Hayes	1876-1880	Rep.	Compromise 1877/Reconstruction Ends.
20. James Garfield	1880-1881	Rep.	Killed.

President	Term	Party	Major Event\Dev
21. Chester Arthur	1881-1884	Rep.	Pendleton Act.
22. Grover Cleveland	1884-1888	Demo.	First Democrat since War; Problem: Surplus funds.
23. Benjamin Harrison	1888-1892	Rep.	Builds up navy.
24. Grover Cleveland	1892-1896	Demo.	Non-consecutive term; Depression 1893.
25. William McKinley	1896-1901	Rep.	Spanish-American War; Killed.
26. Theodore Roosevelt	1901-1908	Rep.	Trust Buster; Square Deal; Big Stick.
27. William Taft	1908-1912	Rep.	Dollar Diplomacy; Splits with T.R.
28. Woodrow Wilson	1912-1920	Demo.	World War I; League of Nations fight.
29. Warren Harding	1920-1923	Rep.	Normalcy; Scandals; Died in office.
30. Calvin Coolidge	1923-1928	Rep.	Pro-business; *laissez faire* administration.
31. Herbert Hoover	1928-1932	Rep.	Depression hits; Rugged Individualism.
32. Franklin Roosevelt	1932-1945	Demo.	New Deal; WWII; Four terms.
33. Harry Truman	1945-1952	Demo.	Fair Deal; Cold War; Korean War; Upset '48.
34. Dwight Eisenhower	1952-1960	Rep.	End Korean War; Modern Republicanism.
35. John Kennedy	1960-1963	Demo.	New Frontier; Bay of Pigs; Missile Crisis; Killed in 1963.
36. Lyndon Johnson	1963-1968	Demo.	Great Society; Vietnam War.
37. Richard Nixon	1968-1974	Rep.	Ends Vietnam War; Watergate; Resigns.

Great Presidents of the United States

Presidents	Domestic Success	Foreign Success	Lasting Impact on Country/Presidency
George Washington	• Bill of Rights approved. • National Bank begun. • Taxing authority established. • Government authority established (Whiskey Rebellion).	• Jay Treaty; British cut of forts in Northwest. • Neutrality in European War. • Farewell Address (no entangling alliances). • Treaty of San Lorenzo (opened the Mississippi River).	• Created/established office of President. • Sound financial footing created. • Isolationism towards Europe. • Secured the "West" (area beyond the Appalachian Mts).
Thomas Jefferson	• Lobbied Congress to pass his program. • Abolished Whiskey tax. • Reduced national debt. • Pardon Sedition violators. • Judicial reform.	• Louisiana Purchase • Barbary Pirate Wars • Kept U.S. out of European War.	• Transition from Federalists was peaceful/positive. • Expanded territory of U.S.A. • Promoted rights rather than control of people.
Abraham Lincoln	• Preserved Union. • Emancipation proclamation/13th amendment. • Homestead Act. • Reformed banking system.	• Kept Europe out of Civil War. • Forced France out of Mexico.	• Kept nation whole. • Gave nation a new birth of freedom. • Expanded president's war-making powers.
Franklin Roosevelt	• New Deal Reforms. • Social Security. • Assisted homeless and unemployed. • Federal Deposit Insurance Corp. • Security Exchange Commission.	• Led U.S. through World War II. • Established United Nations. • Led U.S. from isolationism to internationalism.	• America became a superpower. • Government expanded role in time of crisis. • Focus attention and power in the Oval Office.

Historical Periods

By AP test time in May, most students have been bombarded by hundreds of facts and dates. In this blizzard of information, it is possible to lose track of the broad delineations of United States history. On the AP test, however, there will often be essay questions or multiple choice questions that refer to a historical period. Unless students are familiar with these eras, they may misinterpret or incorrectly answer a question that otherwise they could easily master.

The following chart presents the major historical periods of United States history. In addition it identifies the events that marked the beginning and ending of the era. Students might review the chart by looking at a list of events and placing them in their appropriate historical period. This will develop a stronger chronological sense and decrease the likelihood of seeing unfamiliar time references on the AP test.

Historical Periods

Period	Date	Events
Colonial Era	1607-1763	1. Jamestown Founded 2. French/Indian War ended
Revolutionary Era	1763-1783	1. England ended salutary neglect 2. Treaty of Paris signed
Confederation Era	1781-1789	1. States surrendered land claims 2. Constitution ratified
Era of Good Feelings	1815-1824	1. War of 1812 ended 2. Election of 1824
Jacksonian Era	1828-1848	1. Andrew Jackson elected president 2. Mexican War ended
Antebellum Period (South before Civil War)	1800-1861	1. Cotton gin developed 2. Civil War started
Reconstruction Era	1865-1877	1. Civil War ended 2. Compromise of 1877
Gilded Age	1868-1901	1. Ulysses Grant elected president 2. Death of William McKinley
Progressive Era	1901-1914	1. Square Deal started 2. World War I began in Europe
New Deal Era	1932-1939	1. F. Roosevelt elected president 2. World War I began in Europe
Fair Deal Era	1945-1953	1. F.D.R. died/Harry Truman became president 2. Korean War divided nation
New Frontier/Great Society	1960-1969	1. John Kennedy elected president 2. Vietnam War divided nation

Coming of American Revolution

Although the first shots of the American Revolution were fired in 1775, trouble between England and its colonies had been building for many years. With the end of the French and Indian war, the British abandoned "salutary neglect" and began to tighten their control over the thirteen colonies. England hoped to raise revenue in America to pay down their national debt and to provide for colonial defenses. Britain proposed to do this through a series of revenue acts and policies designed to tighten the mercantile system.

The following chart traces the British attempt to bring the American colonies closer to the empire after 1763. As you study it, consider whether, given the British mercantile system and the colonial mind set of the 1760s and 1770s, the American Revolution could have been avoided.

Coming of the American Revolution

Act or Activity	Background	Provisions	Colonial Reaction	British Reaction
Proclamation Line of 1763	• British hoped to pacify Indians in "west." • Prevented stationing of troops on frontier.	• Forbade settlement west of Appalachian Mountains. • Everyone there must return.	• Anger. • Continued to settle in the area.	• British repealed it by the Treaty of Fort Stanwick 1768.
Sugar Act 1764	• Raise money for colonial defense.	• Duty on foreign molasses reduced but would now be enforced.	• Anger. • Smuggled.	• Attempted to enforce tax.
Stamp Act 1765	• Raise money. • Same tax existed in Great Britain.	• Taxed dice, playing cards, newspapers, marriage licenses. Fifty items taxed in all.	• Called Stamp Congress. • Petitioned the King. • Urban riots. • Non-importation. • Said it was an internal tax.	• Repealed law. • No money raised.
Declaratory Act 1765	• When Stamp Act repealed, British needed to save face.	• England could pass any laws for the colonies	• Ignored it.	• N.A.
Townshend Act 1767	• Raise money. • Regulate trade. • External tax.	• Taxed imports: glass, paint, white lead, paper, tea.	• Boycott. • Urban riots.	• Repealed taxes on everything but tea in 1770.
Boston Massacre 1770	• Troops in city to enforce laws.	• N.A.	• Confronted soldiers.	• Opened fire on mob, five colonials killed.
Boston Tea Party 1773	• Colonists wanted to protest tea tax.	• Tax on tea from 1770.	• Boycott of tea. • Sons of Liberty threw 342 cases of tea into Boston Harbor.	• Intolerable or Coercive Acts passed.
First Continental Congress 1774	• Met to decide how to help Massachusetts fight the Coercive Acts.	• N.A.	• Petitioned King. • Boycotted British goods. • Called for second Congress in May 1775.	• Put troops in cities. • Decided to hold firm.

The National Banks

The National Banks of the United States dominated American economic history from 1790-1844. No issue was more contentious between the Federalists and Republicans as they established the financial foundations of the nation. In the early years of the republic, Alexander Hamilton's supporters clashed with Thomas Jefferson's supporters over the Bank's constitutionality and its inherent unfairness to the poor.

Later, when the Bank was re-chartered, it became a raging controversy between the Jacksonian Democrats and Henry Clay's Whigs. Further it divided the country geographically as western farmers blamed the Bank for their economic woes and saw it as a symbol of eastern financial elitism and dominance over them.

The following chart summarizes the First and Second Banks of the United States. It can be used in conjunction with Lesson 7 on political parties. As you study the Bank, consider why it was so controversial. Can you think of any other economic issue that so dominated United States history?

First and Second National Banks

	1st	2nd
Years	1791-1811	1816-1836
Reason for Creation	• Hamilton modeled it after Bank of England. • Paid dividends, and interest to government—source of revenue.	• 1811-1816 country in economic chaos. • Explosion in number of state banks.
Function	• Flexible currency. • Adequate credit for business. • Revenue for national government.	• Curtailed state banks. • Flexible currency. • Adequate credit. • Contain inflation. • Restrain land speculation.
Supporters	• Federalist Party. • Mercantile groups.	• Madison signed re-charter • National Republicans/Whigs. • Henry Clay/Nicholas Biddle.
Opponents	• Republican Party. • Backcountry farmers. • States right's supporters.	• Old Jeffersonians. • Andrew Jackson—Democrats. • Western farmers.
Reason for Demise	• Republicans in power in 1811 • Madison's government would not renew charter.	• Jackson's veto. • Became a haven for opponents to Jackson. • Undemocratic in egalitarian 1830s.
Constitutional Issue	• Federalist: Bank "necessary and proper" in Constitution. • Republicans: Violated Constitution—not in Article 1, Section 8. • Great Struggle of Loose vs. Strict Interpretation of the Constitution.	• 1818, *McCulloch vs. Maryland* declared Bank constitutional. • 1832 in his veto message Jackson declared Bank unconstitutional.

Liberal and Conservative in United States History

Two of the most misunderstood political terms in the United States history are liberal and conservative. Basically liberals promote and encourage change while conservatives accept the *status quo* and support only small, incremental changes. Yet the two terms have a perplexing way of confusing students. Part of the difficulty is their meanings have flip-flopped throughout the decades. For example the liberalism of the Jeffersonians in the early nineteenth century became, in part, the conservative beliefs of the last twenty-five years of the century. And Alexander Hamilton's conservative ideas of expanding the governmental role in society in the 1790s to promote public interest was warmly endorsed by the liberals in the 1930s.

The following chart will help you focus on the shifting nature of liberal and conservative labels from 1790-1940. As you study it, try to formulate a clearer definition of liberals and conservatives. Also consider why the terms have changed their meaning so often in the course of United States history.

Changing Definition of Liberal and Conservative

Liberal	Conservative
1790-1824 • Jefferson spokesman • Favored farmers • Best government is least government • States' rights • Opposed National Bank • Low taxes/tariff • Weak defense • *Laissez Faire*	• Hamilton spokesman • Commercial groups • Government needs energy • Centralized power • Favored Bank • Tariff necessary • Strong defense
1824-1840 • Pro-union • States' rights on roads/canals • Strong President • Anti-Bank • Jacksonians	• Compact theory of government • Favored national program of roads/canals • Weak President • Pro-Bank • Whigs/Henry Clay
1840-1860 • Pro-union • Anti-slavery • National program of roads and canals • Pro-National Bank • Anti-expansion • Opposed slavery in territories	• States' rights • Pro-slavery • Opposed national program roads/canals • Favored independent treasury system • Favored expansion • Favored slavery in territories
1870-1900 • Honesty in government • Reform Darwinism • Anti-imperialism • Mugwumps, Half Breeds • Expanded money supply • Government regulation of railroad/*businesses* • Low tariffs	• Spoils system • Social Darwinism • Expansionist • Stalwarts (Rep.), Bourbons (Dem.) • Gold standard • *Laissez-faire* • High tariffs • Gospel of Wealth
1900-1940 • Government intervention • Progressives • Regulations of Trusts • Collective security • Consumer protection • T. Roosevelt, F.D.R., W. Wilson • Direct relief in 1930s • New Deal, Square Deal • New Nationalism/Freedom • Low tariffs	• *Laissez-faire* • Old Guard • Hands off business • Isolationism • Taft, Lodge, Harding, Coolidge, Hoover • Rugged Individualism • Normalcy in 1920s • Best government is least government • High tariffs

Political Parties in the Nineteenth Century

The Founding Fathers dreaded the formation of political parties in America. They feared that "factions" would corrupt and compromise the integrity of the government. Men such as James Madison and George Washington believed that political parties would undermine the crucial element of a successful republic—the virtue of the people. Nevertheless parties formed quickly. Disagreements over the financial plan, the nature of the Constitution, and the English-French conflict of the 1790s gave rise to the Federalist and Republican parties. Thus, despite the hopes of some of the Founding Fathers, the United States developed a political party system.

The following charts present the principles of the political parties and traces their evolution in the nineteenth century. Because the parties divided themselves into conservative and liberal positions, these materials should be used in conjunction with Lesson 6. As you study these charts, think about the political issues that have consistently divided Americans in their history and whether parties serve any useful function in our political system.

Political Parties in the Nineteenth Century

Democratic Republicans	Federalists
• Leader Thomas Jefferson	• Leader Alexander Hamilton
• Weak central government	• Strong central government
• Conserve states' rights	• Reduce states' rights
• Strict view of Constitution	• Loose view of Constitution
• Agrarian oriented	• Business oriented
• Low taxes	• High taxes
• Weak military	• Strong military
• Anti-National Bank	• Pro-National Bank
• Pro-French	• Pro-British
Jacksonian Democrats	**Whigs**
• Jeffersonian traditions	• Hamiltonian traditions
• Small farmers/mechanics	• Mercantile/business interest
• Anti-National Bank	• Pro-National Bank
• State control of roads and canals	• National government builds roads and canals (American System)
• Pro-slavery	• Opposed spread of slavery
• Pro-Mexican War	• Anti-Mexican War
• Strong executive	• Weak executive
• *Laissez-faire*	• Energetic national government
Democrats (1865-1900)	**Republicans (1865-1900)**
• Blamed for Civil War (Bloody Shirt)	• Opposed secession
• States' rights	• Opposed the spread of slavery
• Agrarian oriented	• Whig influence/pro-business
• Feared strong central government	• Supported active national government
• Supported Gold Standard	• Supported Gold Standard
• Used spoils system	• Used spoils system
• Supported lowering tariffs (1887)	• Supported high tariffs
• Reduced government role in railroads	• Government support for development

Evolution of the Two-Party System

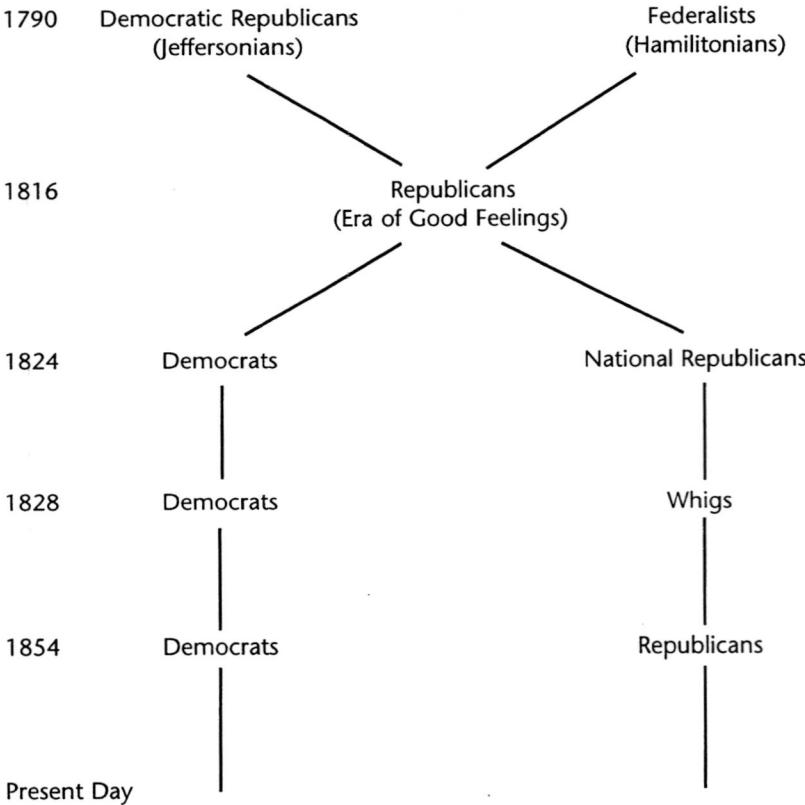

Freedom of the Seas and Wars with Europe

The United States has always defended it's right to sail the seas. In exercising this right, however, America had difficulty from time to time. It became especially troublesome for the United States when our claim to maritime freedom intruded into general wars in Europe. In 1793 and 1796, George Washington proclaimed that during European conflicts, America would avoid political and military alliances but would continue traveling the seas and maintain commercial relations with all nations (See Lesson 11). This policy, while prudent, led to war on two occasions. In 1812 and 1917, events forced the United States to abandon its isolationism to defend its rights by force.

The following chart outlines the background and events that led to American entry into war in 1812 and 1917. As you review it and the chart in Lesson 11, assess the wisdom of America's decision to remain neutral and, at the same time, travel unimpeded into the European war zone. What factors did our leaders consider when they formulated and followed this policy? How did they define our national interest in 1812 and 1917?

Freedom of the Seas 1812 and 1917

	War of 1812	World War I
Background	• France/England went to war in 1793 • Both countries asked U.S. for assistance. • U.S. refused, both seized our ships. • England seized our men.	• Central Powers fought Triple Entente. • Both Germany/England blockaded their enemy. • German submarines sunk American shipping. • England searched American ships.
Presidents	• T. Jefferson/J. Madison	• Woodrow Wilson.
Attempts to Stay Neutral	Withheld trade by: • Embargo Act 1807. • Non-Intercourse Act 1809. • Macon Bill #2 1810.	• Neutrality Proclamation. • *Lusitania* protest note. • *Sussex* Pledge.
Major Events	• *Chesapeake-Leopard* Clash in 1807. • 1000s of men impressed by British. • 100s of American ships searched.	• *Lusitania* sunk 1915. • *Sussex* pledge 1916. • Zimmerman Note 1917. (German proposed alliance with Mexico.)
Outcome	• War declared against England in June 1812.	• War declared against Germany in April 1917.
Comments	• War supported in South/West by War Hawks. • New England shippers opposed "Mr. Madison's War."	• Wilson's strict accountability led to war with Germany. • England seized many ships but did not take lives. • War waged "to make world safe for democracy."

Compromises and the Union

Early American democracy was built on compromise. The first hundred years of American history saw four major compromises enacted to create and to preserve the Union. The issue of congressional representation, slavery, and Reconstruction seriously threatened our domestic tranquility. In each occasion, however, a compromise was enacted which defused the crisis.

The following chart offers an overview of the four major compromises in United States history through Reconstruction. As you review the chart, you might consider whether a democratic republic is more dependent on compromises than other forms of government. You might also speculate as to what consequences would have resulted had the compromises failed.

Compromises and the Union

	Great Compromise 1787	Missouri Compromise	Compromise of 1850	Compromise of 1877
Issue	• Representation in Congress.	• Admission of Missouri to Union would disrupt Senate balance.	• Admission of California. • Disposition of Mexican Cession.	• Presidential victor in 1876.
Background	• Virginia Plan called for representation by population. • New Jersey Plan proposed equal representation.	• Missouri wanted to become the Twelfth slave state. • Would slavery go north of Ohio River? • What would happen to rest of Louisiana Territory?	• Would slavery go into the Mexican Cession? • Should D.C. outlaw the slave trade? • Should Fugitive Slave Law be strengthened? • What would be California status?	• Three states sent two sets of election returns. • Tilden needed only one vote to win. • Commission gave all dispute votes to Hayes.
Elements	• Two houses of Congress. • House based on population. • Senate—two from each state. • Combined VA/NJ plan.	• Missouri became a slave state. • Maine became a free state. • No slavery north of 36° 30' in Louisiana Territory.	• California became free. • Utah/New Mexico organized by popular sovereignty. • Stronger Fugitive Slave Law. • Ended slave trade in D.C.	• Hayes got President. • Garfield made Speaker of House. • Removal of troops from South. • Aid for southern railroad. • Two southerners in Cabinet.
Significance	• Allowed Constitution to be written/approved.	• Postponed the debate over spread of slavery for thirty years.	• Postponed Civil War for ten years.	• Ended Congressional Reconstruction.

The Marshall Court and the National Period

The Federalist party lost political influence in America after the election of 1796. They lost the White House in 1800 when Thomas Jefferson defeated John Adams. The War of 1812 further weakened their political strength until, by its end, the Federalists represented only one-third of the Senate and House. Finally, in the election of 1820, no Federalist candidate challenged James Monroe for the presidency. Thus, during the Era of Good Feelings (a.k.a. the National Period), the Federalists ceased to be a political force.

Yet their political ideology reached beyond 1820. The judiciary branch became a Federalist bastion from 1801 to 1835. The principal reason for this was the work of John Marshall. Appointed to the court in 1801 by John Adams, he served as Chief Justice until 1835. Throughout this time, he championed the twin Federalist goals of strengthening the central government and promoting business interest.

The Federalist philosophy was alive and well during the Era of Good Feelings (1816-1824). Three court decisions in particular demonstrated how the Court strengthened nationalism and encouraged business development. The following chart summarized these three important cases.

As you study the chart, think about how Marshall, the lone Federalist on the Court for most of his tenure, could lead in a Republican era. Further how did the Court "follow the election returns from 1816-1824"?

Rulings of the Marshall Court in the National Period

Case	Ruling	Business Interest Promoted	States' Rights Diminished
Darthmouth College Case 1819	New Hampshire could not revoke college charter because charter was form of contract.	Contract law strengthened.	New Hampshire could not change college from private to public.
McCulloch vs. Maryland 1819	Affirmed bank's constitutionality. Bank cannot be taxed by state.	Upheld bank.	Maryland taxing power diminished.
Gibbon vs. Ogden 1824	New York could not grant a monopoly to steamboat company on Hudson River.	Strengthened federal government power over interstate commerce.	New York's power to regulate trade diminished.

Cornerstones of United States Foreign Policy

In the course of its existence, the United States has established consistent principles of behavior towards various parts of the world. This consistency has been a function of geography, domestic politics, and regional overseas exigencies. Over the last 200 years, America built three distinct foreign policies in Europe, Asia, and South America. The following chart gives an overview of the cornerstones of United States foreign policy—isolationism in Europe, the Monroe Doctrine in South America, and the Open Door in Asia.

As you study this chart, consider two questions. How did the United States define it national interest in each of the three areas of the world? Are there consistent threads of interest that run through all aspects of American foreign policy?

Cornerstones of United States Foreign Policy

	Isolationism	Monroe Doctrine	Open Door
Area of World	Europe.	Western Hemisphere.	Asia.
Year Established	1793.	1823.	1899-1900.
Author	George Washington.	James Monroe, John Quincy Adams.	John Hay.
Background	• Proposed when England/France went to war. • Both countries expected our help.	• Feared Spanish recolonization in South America. • Feared Russian colonies on west coast of U.S.	• Feared Europe would divide China's land. • Feared Europe would create trading spheres.
Elements	• No entangling military or political alliances. • Europe/U.S. have separate spheres of interest. • Commercial relations continued.	• No new colonies in Western Hemisphere. • Existing colonies left alone by U.S. • Isolationism from Europe repeated. • Discourage extension of monarchies into Americas.	• All countries share equal trading rights with China. • All countries guaranteed China's territorial integrity.
Comments	• Resulted in war in 1812, 1917. • Established policy that lasted until 1949 when we joined N.A.T.O.	• England enforced it for seventy years. • Roosevelt Corollary strengthened it in 1904: —U.S. became policeman in Caribbean. —"Big Stick" to keep out all European influence.	• U.S. became protector of China. • Japan closed open door in 1930s in China. • When U.S. challenged Japan, Pearl Harbor hit.

Expansion of the United States 1783-1853

One of the constant themes of American history in the first half of the nineteenth century was the nation's relentless march westward. Expansion was a goal coveted by almost every president from George Washington to Abraham Lincoln. And, where circumstances allowed, America expanded and added territory.

Although the acquisitions were sought to strengthen and unite the nation, they eventually divided and disputed the country. By the 1840s and 1850s, Manifest Destiny, with its call for an empire from ocean to ocean, became intertwined with slavery, and this tore the country apart and brought on the Civil War.

As you examine the chart and map of United States expansion, think about the factors that drove American expansion. Try to list them in order of importance and defend the hierarchy you have established.

Expansion of the United States 1783-1853

Land Area	Date	Means of Acquisition	Cost	Significance
Original thirteen states and area east of Mississippi River	1783	Treaty of Paris with England.	0	• U.S. gained trans-Appalachian empire. • Gateway to land beyond Mississippi River.
Louisiana	1803	Treaty with France.	$15 million	• Gave U.S. control of Mississippi River. • Doubled size of U.S.
Florida	1819	Adams-Onis Treaty with Spain.	$5 million	• Secured southern boundary. • Spain recognized United States claims on Pacific coast.
Oregon	1846	Treaty with England.	0	• Prevented war with England. • Gave U.S. clear claim to land on Pacific coast.
Mexican Cession	1848	Treaty of Guadalupe Hidalgo settled the Mexican War.	$15 million	• Gave U.S. California. • Completed Manifest Destiny.
Gadsden Purchase	1853	Treaty with Mexico.	$10 million	• Bought with hope of building trans-continental railroad in the South.

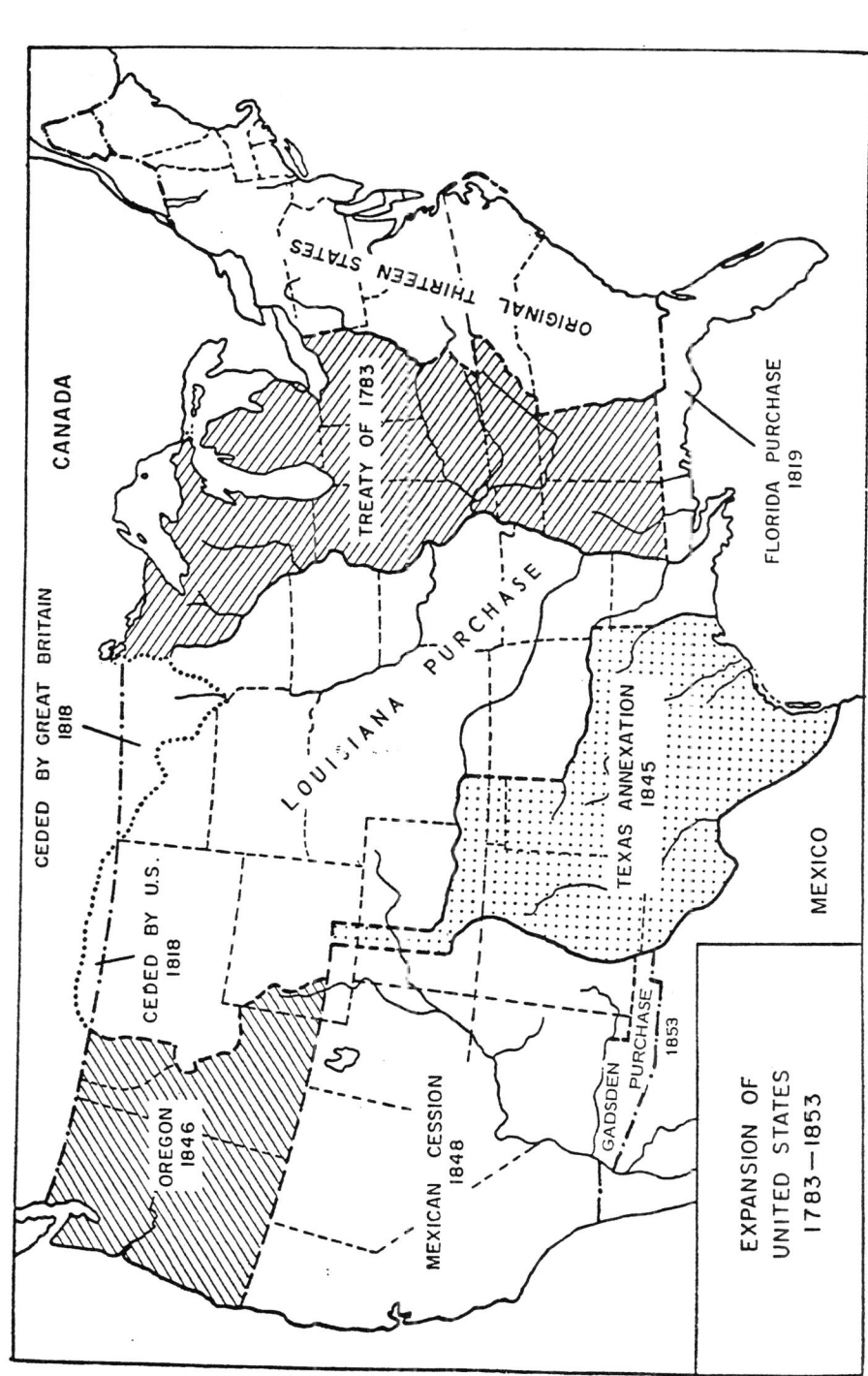

Wars in United States History

While in the United States has professed its dedication to peace, much of its history has been shaped by armed conflicts with other countries. Most of the nineteenth-century clashes resulted from America's attempt to establish and enhance its place in the world. On the other hand, as it matured in the twentieth century, the United States fought principally to maintain its position in the world community.

The following two charts present the eight wars the United States has been involved in its 200-year history. The chart should be studied in conjunction with Lesson 8 (Freedom of the Seas), Lesson 12 (Expansion of the United States), and Lesson 17 (Major Treaties).

As you study the two charts, compare the wars of the nineteenth century with the wars of the twentieth century. What similarities do you see in them? What differences do you notice? How did America's opponents change in the two centuries? How were the causes of the conflicts transformed? Would you have difficulty defending the proposition that Americans are a peaceful people?

Nineteenth Century Wars

	War of 1812	Mexican War	Civil War	Spanish-American War
Dates	1812-1814	1846-1848	1861-1865	1898
President	Madison	Polk	Lincoln	McKinley
Causes	• Impressment. • Freedom of Seas threatened.	• Manifest Destiny. • Texas boundary dispute.	• Eleven southern states withdrew from Union.	• Revolt in Cuba. • *Maine* blew up.
Important Military Events	• Burning of Washington. • New Orleans.	• Buena Vista. • Mexico City.	• Antietam. • Gettysburg. • Vicksburg.	• Manila Bay. • San Juan Hill.
Treaty	• Ghent	• Guadalupe Hidalgo	• Appomattox	• Paris
Terms	• No territory changed hands.	• U.S. got Mexican Cession. • Agreement on Texas border.	• South gave up.	• U.S. got Guam Puerto Rico, Philippines. • Cuba free from Spain.
Importance	• War promoted American nationalism. • Era of Good Feelings began.	• Completed Manifest Destiny. • Re-opened debate over expansion of slavery.	• Union saved. • Bloodiest war in U.S. history.	• U.S. became world, colonial power.

Twentieth Century Wars

	World War I	World War II	Korean War	Vietnam
Dates	1917-1918	1941-1945	1950-1953	1950-1975
President	Wilson	F. Roosevelt Truman	Truman Eisenhower	Truman to Ford
Causes	• German submarine warfare. • Sinking of *Lusitania*.	• Japan closed Open Door in China. • Pearl Harbor attacked. • Germany declared war on U.S.A.	• Communist North attacked South Korea.	• Division of Vietnam caused communist insurgency in South.
Important Military Events	• Belleau Wood. • Chateau Thierry.	• Guadalcanal. • Midway. • El Alamein. • Stalingrad.	• Pusan. • Inchon.	• Gulf of Tonkin. • Pleiku. • Tet Attack.
Treaty	Versailles.	Accord with Axis powers.	Panmunjom Accords.	Paris Accords.
Terms	• Germany surrendered. • League of Nations created.	• Unconditional surrender.	• South Korea remained independent. • Communist remained in the North.	• Cease-fire. • Americans withdrawn. • South Vietnam remained independent.
Importance	• Four Empires destroyed. • Communists took over Russia. • U.S. retreated to isolationism.	• Atomic Age began at Hiroshima. • U.S.S.R./U.S.A. began the Cold War.	• First test of military containment. • First limited war.	• War divided U.S. • 1975 North took over South Vietnam.

Amendments to the Constitution

The Amendments to the Constitution are an important but sometimes overlooked aspect of the United States history survey course. Usually students examine the first ten amendments in conjunction with the struggle over the ratification of the Constitution in 1788-1789. The opponents of the Constitution complained that the document lacked a Bill of Rights and demanded this omission be corrected in order for ratification to proceed. Amendments also figured prominently in the United States history during Reconstruction (1865-1877) and in the early 1920s.

The following is a quick summary of the twenty-seven amendments to the Constitution. As you study them, consider several questions. First, how did the first ten amendments reflect American anxieties about government that developed during the colonial and revolutionary periods? Secondly, how were the Thirteenth, Fourteenth, and Fifteenth amendments the most "revolutionary" of all the changes to the Constitution? Finally, how did the Eighteenth and Nineteenth amendments represent both an extension and a termination of Progressive reforms?

Amendments to Constitution

1. Freedom of religion, speech, assembly.
2. Right to bear arms.
3. Prohibits housing of troops in private homes.
4. Prohibits unreasonable search and seizure.
5. Prohibits double jeopardy, self-incrimination, seizing of property without due process, and just compensation.
6. Right to speedy and public trial; informed of charges against you.
7. Right to jury trial.
8. Prohibits excessive bail; cruel and unusual punishment.
9. Rights not enumerated remain the people's.
10. Powers not delegated to federal government reserved to the states.
11. Federal courts have no authority in suits by citizens against a state.
12. Separate electoral voting for President and Vice President.
13. Ended slavery in U.S.
14. Blacks given citizenship; federal government protects rights if state fails to do so.
15. Black men given right to vote.
16. Congress can levy income tax.
17. Direct election of Senator.
18. Prohibited the manufacture, sale, and transportation of liquor.
19. Women given right to vote.
20. Congress starts on January 3. President starts on January 20 of year following their election.
21. Repealed Eighteenth Amendment.
22. Limited president to two terms or ten years.
23. District of Columbia got three electoral votes in presidential election.
24. Abolished poll taxes.
25. When president dies or disabled vice-president becomes president; new vice-president appointed; established procedures in case of presidential disability.
26. Eighteen-year-olds given right to vote.
27. Congress prohibited from changing its pay during a congressional term.

The Abolitionist Movement

The period from 1830-1860 was a time of social and political reform in the United States. Reformers such as Dorothea Dix, Horace Mann, and Elizabeth Cady Stanton attempted to change the way the country treated the mentally ill, educated its children, and viewed women. All these efforts, however, were dwarfed by the attempt to end slavery. Prodded by the British anti-slavery movement, Americans began establishing abolitionist societies in the early 1830s. The American abolitionist movement was united for a brief period of time, but by the early 1840s fissures appeared.

The following chart outlines the three distinct strands of the abolitionist crusade. As you look at the chart, consider how the abolitionists found common areas of agreement yet disagreed over the means to their ends.

The Abolitionist Movement

	American Colonization Society	American Anti-Slavery Society	American/Foreign Anti-Slavery Society
Date Started	1817	1833	1840
Leaders	Robert Finley, Henry Clay, James Madison.	William Garrison.	Theodore Weld, Lewis/Arthur Tappan.
Goals	Return freed people to Africa.	Immediate, uncompensated, end to all slaves.	Gradual end to slavery with some compensation.
Means	Lobby Congress for support.	Moral persuasion, speeches, articles in *The Liberator*	Moral persuasion, political pressure.
Women's Role	N.A.	Full, equal participation.	Limited role, mostly work behind scenes support the men.
Summary	Established Liberia 1823. About fifteen thousand freed people returned to Africa. Freed people opposed the organization.	Controversial, confrontational; challenged churches, Constitution, even the Union itself.	Thought Garrison too extreme. Broke with him in 1840. More moderate, more political.

Women's Movement in the Nineteenth Century

The Nineteenth Century witnessed many attempts to reform and improve America. One of the most controversial of these reforms was the women's movement. The women who led this crusade came mainly from the ranks of the abolitionists. In fact, before the Civil War, the two most significant women leaders, Elizabeth Cady Stanton and Lucretia Mott, focused their efforts mainly on the battle against slavery.

In addition to their divided attentions, women faced other hurdles in their quest for full citizenship. There were legal barriers that prevented women from voting or serving on jury. Further laws of coverture gave husbands complete control over their wives economic life.

Moreover women had to combat not only legal obstacles but psychological barriers as well. Most women accepted their place and status in American society. Stanton, Mott, and others had great difficulty raising women's awareness to the injustice of a male-dominated society.

The following chart outlines the three major strands of the women's movement in the nineteenth century. As you study it identify the issues that united women and the ones that divided them. Also why did women target suffrage as their primary goal?

Women's Movement in the Nineteenth Century

	Seneca Falls Movement	National Women's Suffrage Association	American Women's Suffrage Association
Leaders	• Elizabeth C. Stanton. • Lucretia Mott.	• E.C. Stanton. • Susan B. Anthony.	• Lucy Stone.
Goals	• Right to vote. • Lessening coverture. • Overcome "Cult of Domesticity"/true womanhood.	• Right to vote along with black men. • Include women in Fifteenth Amendment. • Wide range of reforms.	• Gradual pressure for women's right to vote. • Accept Fifteenth Amendment as for black men only.
Supporters	• Middle class • Male abolitionists. • Quakers.	• Young, educated women. • Many from Seneca Falls. • Women in western states. • Only women officials.	• Less radical women. • Boston-bred women • Abolitionists: F. Douglass. • Welcomed male members.
Methods	• Published Declaration of Sentiments. • Held annual convention through the beginning of the Civil War.	• Lobbied for Amendment giving women the right to vote.	• State-by-state approach to achieving the vote. • Avoid reforms not related to suffrage.

Major Treaties in U.S. History

As America explained and became involved in world affairs, conflicts arose. To resolve some of these disputes, American diplomats sought agreements and treaties. The following chart summarizes the major international agreements in which the United States was involved from 1794-1954.

Students should use the chart in conjunction with Lessons 8, 11, 12, and 13. Collectively the charts describe many aspects of American diplomatic and military history. As you review these materials, evaluate the proposition that, in the long run, America accomplished more at the negotiating table than on the battlefield.

Selected United States Treaties

Treaty Date	Nations	Provisions
Jay Treaty 1794-1795	U.S./England	1. Britain left forts in N.W. USA. 2. Arbitration over war debts.
Treaty of Ghent 1814	U.S./England	1. Ended War of 1812/No land changes. 2. No mention of British impressment.
Adams/Onis 1819	U.S./Spain	1. U.S. got Florida; U.S. paid $5 million. 2. U.S. gave up claim to Texas. 3. Spain recognized U.S. claim to west coast Oregon country/U.S. now had a Pacific coast claim.
Treaty of Guadalupe Hidalgo 1848	U.S./Mexico	1. Mexico recognized Rio Grande border. 2. Mexico gave up Mexican Cession. 3. U.S. paid Mexico $15 million.
Treaty of Paris 1898	U.S./Spain	1. Ended Spanish American war. 2. Cuba freed from Spain. 3. U.S. got Puerto Rico, Guam. 4. U.S. paid $20 million for Philippines.
Treaty of Versailles 1919	Allies/Germany	1. Ended W.W. I 2. Established the League of Nations. 3. Germany punished for starting war. 4. U.S. Senate rejected treaty because of League and isolationist feelings in USA.
North Atlantic Treaty Organization 1949	U.S./Twelve European Countries	1. Attempt to contain Communism in Europe. 2. An attack on one is attack on all. 3. Collective Security. 4. First entangling alliance for the U.S.
Southeast Asia Treaty Organization 1954	U.S., Great Britain, France, Australia, New Zealand, Thailand, Pakistan, Philippines.	1. Repel common danger in the region. 2. Civil wars aided communist causes. 3. Helped Vietnam, Laos, Cambodia. 4. Containment of communism in Asia.

Reconstruction of the South

When the Civil War ended in 1865, many questions arose about the political and physical rebuilding of the eleven southern states which attempted to leave the Union in 1861. Over the next three years, the country was convulsed in conflict about Reconstruction. The most contentious issue of the era was the futures of the former slaves. The overriding theme of this struggle was whether President Andrew Johnson or the Radical Republicans would decide the fate of the defeated South and the freed people.

The political battle became so heated that in 1868, President Johnson was impeached. Although they could not convict him, the Radical Republicans did gain control of Reconstruction and attempted to revolutionize social and political relationships in the United States.

The following chart offers a concise summary of the major issues and elements of the competing Reconstruction plans. As you study the chart, think about how the plans would appeal to the following groups: Freedmen, southern planters, northern Democrats, poor southern whites, moderate northern Republicans, abolitionists, western farmers, and northern factory workers.

Reconstruction Plans

	Presidential	Congressional
Who was in charge?	President	Congress.
Dates	April-December 1865.	1865-1877.
Had States Left the Union?	No, need to restore states to "proper relationship with the union."	Yes, conquered territories.
Acts	• Proclamation of Amnesty and Reconstruction 1863, 1865.	• Civil Rights Act 1866. • Fourteenth Amendment 1868. • Reconstruction Acts 1867-1868. • Fifteenth Amendment 1870. • Force Acts 1870-1871 • Civil Rights Act 1875.
Elements of Plans	• Renounce secession. • Ratify Thirteenth Amendment. • 10% of voters from 1860 swear allegiance to Union. • Confederate officers, officials, rich must make special request for pardon.	• Ratify Thirteenth, Fourteenth, Fifteenth Amendments. • Accept black citizenship. • Black men suffrage. • Military occupation of South. • Confederate officials, officers, soldiers could not vote. • Civil Rights Act 1875.
Aid for Freedmen	• None, states rights emphasized.	• Freedman's Bureau provided welfare, education. • Voting protection. • No permanent land distribution.

The Judicial Road to *Plessy*

When the Supreme Court ruled in 1896 that "separate but equal" facilities for blacks and whites were constitutional, the ruling culminated the court's role in gradually narrowing the interpretation of the Fourteenth Amendment. (See Lesson 14 for a summary of the amendment.) It also gave judicial approval to the Jim Crow system that separated the races in social and cultural settings in the South after the Civil War. The trend of the court's decisions from 1870-1900 was to restrict the scope of the fourteenth Amendment, especially its "equal protection" clause for black Americans. By the time of *Plessy*, the nation was in full retreat from the Reconstruction era pledge that all men were created equal.

The following chart summarizes the four major cases that defined the Court's attitude towards civil rights after the Civil War. In *Plessy* the majority ruled that "legislation is powerless to eradicate racial instincts or to abolish distinctions based upon physical differences...." Can you outline the events from 1877-1896 that gave rise to this line of thinking?

Judicial Road to *Plessy vs. Ferguson*

Case	Date	Background	Questions to be Answered	Ruling
Slaughter House Case	1873	Louisiana created a monopoly in New Orleans. Butchers believed their Fourteenth Amendment rights were violated.	Did Fourteenth Amendment expand the equal protection clause of the Constitution.	• No, defense of rights still a state job. • Thirteenth, Fourteenth Amendment did not greatly expand power of U.S. government. • Fourteenth Amendment did not create new set of citizenship rights.
U.S. vs. Cruikshank	1874	Colfax Massacre resulted in 100 black deaths and 3 white deaths. No one convicted.	Did Fourteenth Amendment protect blacks from private acts of violence?	• No, Fourteenth Amendment did not give U.S. government power to suppress ordinary crimes in a state. • U.S. involved only when state actions denied rights.
U.S. vs. Singleton	1883	Black denied entry to Opera House in New York City.	Did Civil Rights Act/1875 prohibit *private* acts of discrimination?	• No, C.R. Act of 1875 unconstitutional. • Fourteenth Amendment only dealt with state not private acts of discrimination.
Plessy vs. Ferguson	1896	Black tried to sit in "white" railcar to test Louisiana's Jim Crow laws.	Did Jim Crow system violate Fourteenth Amendment?	• No, legislation powerless to stop private acts of racial bias. • Separate facilities were not inherently unconstitutional. • Facilities could be separate but equal.

Black Leaders 1880-1968

As the idealism of the Reconstruction era faded in the mid-1870s, black Americans confronted a betrayal of the promise of equal rights. Increasingly the federal government's support retreated, and America became more hostile towards former slaves and free blacks. By the mid-1880s, Jim Crowism ruled the nation.

Since the early 1880s, black leaders have stepped forward to offer guidance in dealing with the questions of the "color line" in America. Some leaders suggested accommodation and integration while others demanded a more confrontational means of dealing with racial inequalities in America.

The following chart outlines the contribution of five black leaders. As you study the chart, which leaders do you think were most constructive in their approach to the racial problems of their times, and which leaders do you think acted out of frustrations and anger?

Black Leaders 1880-1968

	Message	Supporters	Method	Significance
Booker T. Washington 1856-1915	• Atlanta Compromise: - Accept social/political inequality. - Work for economic equality in farming/trades.	• Southern rural blacks. • Southern whites. • White industrialists.	• Accommodation with whites. • Created Tuskegee Institute. • Blacks/whites remain separate socially.	• Got money for black schools. • Advised presidents. • Secretly worked to overturn segregation.
W.E.B. DuBois 1868-1963	• Talented tenth of blacks must lead. • Strive for full equality.	• Intellectuals. • Urban, northern blacks. • White liberals.	• Helped form NAACP in 1909. • Wrote books to energize blacks.	• Challenged B.T. Washington. • Agitated for equality.
Marcus Garvey 1887-1940	• Black self-sufficiency. • Black pride. • Pride in Africa. • Return to Africa. • Expanded Black capitalism.	• Urban blacks.	• Created Universal Negro Improvement Association. • Formed Black Star Line—black-owned company.	• First leader to talk of black pride. • Linked American blacks to Africa. • Arrested on mail fraud, deported.
Martin Luther King 1929-1968	• Justice by religious, moral means. • Whites must see injustice in Jim Crow.	• Rural, southern, church-going blacks.	• Non-violent protest. • Marches, demonstrations.	• Opened eyes of country to immorality of segregation. • Greatest rights leader of the times.
Malcolm X (Little) 1925-1965	• Black power. • Enemy is white man. • Black nationalism. • Rejected integration. • May have reevaluated his position at end.	• Northern, urban young male.	• Speeches, confrontations with white establishment. • Challenged King.	• Black Muslims identified with revolt in 1960s. • Frightened whites.

Reform Movements
of the Twentieth Century

The great domestic struggle of twentieth century American history has been between the reform impulse and the forces of the *status quo*. The major parameter of this debate was the degree to which the national government ought to involve itself in the social and economic lives of the citizens—the issue of *laissez-faire*. This conflict over government intervention has defined the major issues of twentieth century United States domestic politics.

There have been three attempts to change America in the twentieth century: The Progressive Movement, 1900-1914; the New Deal/Fair Deal of the 1930s and 1940s; and the New Frontier/Great Society programs of the 1960s. The following chart summarizes each of the movements. Historians have noted that these reforms occurred in thirty-year cycles in the twentieth century. That is, a wave of public purpose (reform) was usually followed by a private interest interlude (i.e. 1920s, 1950s, 1970s). What factors can you think of that might explain this cycle of reform?

Reform Movements of the Twentieth Century

	Square Deal/ New Freedom	New Deal	Fair Deal	New Frontier	Great Society
Dates	1900-1914	1933-1938	1949-1953	1961-1963	1963-1968
Presidents	T. Roosevelt W. Taft W. Wilson	F. Roosevelt	H. Truman	J. Kennedy	L. Johnson
Goals	• Control corporation • Consumer protection • Clean up government • Conserve environment	• Relief of unemployed • Reform of financial institutions • Recovery from depression	• Continue New Deal	• Continue New Deal	• Finish New Deal
Examples of Action	• Hepburn Act • Pure Food and Drug Act • Clayton Act • Northern Security Case • Federal Reserve Act • Federal Trade Commission • Newlands Act • Keatings Owens Act	• National Industrial Recovery Act • Agricultural Adjustment Act • Civilian Conservation Corporation • Public Works Administration • Social Security Act • Federal De-posit Insurance Corporation • Tennessee Valley Authority • Security Exchange Commission	• Desegregated Military • Employment Act 1946 • Minimum Wage Raised • Expanded Social Security	• Proposed: Medicare; Civil Rights Act; aid to Education, Mass Transit	• Medicare Act • Civil Right Act • Education Act • Voting Rights Act • Economic Opportunity Act • Housing Act • Higher Education Act • Immigration Act • Highway Safety Act

The Three R's of the New Deal

The New Deal reforms of the 1930s triggered controversy and discussion in the United States about the nature of capitalism and the role of the government in society. For over sixty years, politicians have continued to debate the usefulness and merits of the New Deal. In essence the domestic political dialogue of the last two-thirds of the twentieth century has revolved around the pros and cons of FDR's reform program.

Given its importance, students should have a working knowledge of the three R's of the New Deal—Relief, Recovery, and Reform. The following outline summarizes ten of the most significant New Deal acts. As you look at these areas of New Deal reform, consider the criteria that was used to place an act in one of the three categories. Also which area would you think met with the greatest resistance in the 1930s? Why?

The Three R's of the New Deal

Relief

1. Federal Emergency Relief Administration: Provided money to states for direct relief for the people. Matched funds that states allocated for relief. Replaced in 1935 by Works Progress Administration.
2. Works Progress Administration: Massive and direct relief for the unemployed. Created temporary jobs for unemployed. Included work for teachers, musicians, theater people, and artists.
3. Civilian Works Administration (1933-1934): Designed for emergency relief. Employed more than four million people in temporary, civic improvement jobs.
4. Public Works Administration: Provided temporary jobs. Built highways, parkways, and public buildings.

Recovery

1. National Industrial Recovery Act: Allowed businesses to get together to fix prices, set standards of quality. Also allowed labor to bargain collectively for higher wages. Set up codes of fair competition in industries. Declared unconstitutional in 1935.
2. Agricultural Adjustment Administration: Purpose to balance farm production/consumption. Farmers paid not to produce. Hoped to raise prices by restricting production without lowering farm incomes. Declared unconstitutional in 1935.

Reform

1. Security and Exchange Commission: Regulated Wall Street, watched stock market to prevent another crash. Protected investors from insider manipulation and from misrepresentation in the sale of securities.
2. Federal Deposit Insurance Corporation (Glass Steagall Banking Act): Federal government insured deposits up to $5000. Designed to restore faith in banking system.
3. Social Security: Government sponsored retirement program. Provided unemployment assistance, helped children and widows.
4. Tennessee Valley Authority: Built dams, provided flood control, and electric power for Tennessee River Valley.

American Involvement in Vietnam

The Vietnam War was the most divisive and controversial conflict in post-World War II United States history. It divided America internally and ended with a Communist victory in South Vietnam. Certainly the war was the defining element of American politics from 1965 to 1975.

For AP students, the Vietnam era presents an instructional problem. Most classes are just starting to study the 1960s and the war when the test occurs in mid-May, yet questions about the war often appear on the test. You should be certain that you can identify Ngo Dinh Diem, Ho Chi Minh, The Geneva Conference, Gulf of Tonkin Resolution, Tet Offensive, and Vietnamization as part of your review of the war.

The following outline will help alleviate this problem. It is an overview of America's role in the war. As you study it, look for three or four critical turning points in America's descent into the quagmire of the war. Why did you select these events?

American Role in Vietnam War

1860-1890	France gained control of area known as Indochina (Vietnam, Cambodia, and Laos).
1940-1945	Japan moved into Indochina after Germany conquered France in World War II. U.S. intelligence (O.S.S.) used Ho Chi Minh against the Japanese.
1945-1949	France tried to recolonize Indochina. Ho Chi Minh resisted. U.S. faced a dilemma: Wanted to reduce colonialism in Asia but not at the expense of communist expansion.
1949	Fall of China; U.S. stepped up aid to France against Ho Chi Minh.
1954	Geneva Conference: France leaves Vietnam; Indochina becomes Vietnam, Laos, and Cambodia. Vietnam divided, to hold unification election in 1956.
1954-1956	North Vietnam unified under Ho Chi Minh; South organized by Ngo Diem supported by U.S.A.
1956	U.S. encouraged Diem not to hold elections; U.S. pledged support to keep Communists out.
1956-1961	Viet Cong insurgents work to overthrow Diem; U.S. sent 1,000 advisors and economic help.
1961-1963	JFK resisted sending combat soldiers, but increased advisors (16,000) and economic help.
1963	Diem overthrown by his military and killed.
1964	Political chaos in South; Gulf of Tonkin Resolution: U.S. Congress authorized LBJ "to take all necessary measures to repel any armed attack..." in South Vietnam. Blank check for U.S. involvement.
1964-1965	Political, military chaos in South Vietnam; 1965 U.S. began sending combat soldiers, began bombing North Vietnam.
1967-1968	U.S. embarked on large scale bombing of North; 550,000 combat soldiers on search and destroy missions in South Vietnam.
1968	Tet Offensive: Viet Cong/North Vietnam attack cities and towns in South; American public shocked. LBJ decided not to seek re-election; negotiations began to end U.S. involvement.
1969-1970	Richard Nixon started "Vietnamization": U.S. troops pulled out; increased bombing of North.
1970	U.S. invaded Cambodia to strike at Viet Cong supplies. Set off firestorm of protest in USA.
1973	Peace treaty reached. U.S. pulled out troops.
1975	Viet Cong and North Vietnam launch attack on South Vietnam and overwhelm government.
Today	Vietnam is one country under Communist control.

Containment of Communism

At the end of the Second World War, the tenuous wartime alliance between the United States and Soviet Union broke apart. Unable to agree over the future of Eastern Europe, the two superpowers began a non-shooting competition that columnist Walter Lippman labeled a "Cold War."

The U.S. strategy in this struggle was to contain Communist expansion around the world. Largely influenced by George Kennan's article "The Source of Soviet Conduct" and his Long Telegram, the Truman administration viewed the Soviet Union as an ideological, expansionistic power bent on world conquest. Faced with this formidable enemy, Truman decided to follow the "long-term patient, but firm and vigilant containment of Russian expansion." Although labeled in different ways, and focused on differing geographical regions, this policy became the foundation of U.S. strategy in the Cold War.

The following chart outlines how five administrations approached containment from 1945-1975. As you study this information, consider the following questions. Were there alternatives to containment? What were the domestic political factors that influenced containment? Was containment short-sighted and wasteful or was it why the U.S. won the Cold War?

Containment 1945-1975

Presidents	Strategy	Means	Explanation

Truman	Containment	• Use of economic /military aid.
		• Program
		  -Truman Doctrine
		  -Marshall Plan
		  -N.A.T.O.
		  -Korean War
			• Communist threat in Greece/Turkey prompted U.S. assistance.
			• Sent aid to Europe 1948 to 1954.
			• N.A.T.O.—First entangling alliance for U.S.A.
			• Korea—first limited war.

Eisenhower	"New Look" to contain communism.	• Massive retaliation. • Rollback of communism. • Brinkmanship.	• Relied on air power, nuclear power. • Empty call for freeing communist-dominated areas. • Taking Reds to brink of war if necessary.
Kennedy	"Flexible response to communism." Stand firm in Europe.	• Stop wars of national liberation in third world. • Use U.S. soldiers. • Strong stand in Berlin. • Block communists in Cuba, Vietnam.	• Use guerrilla as well as conventional forces. • Tried to topple Castro. • Bay of Pigs. • Cuban Missile Crisis. • Sent 16,000 troops to Vietnam.
Johnson	Containment in Asia. Stand in Europe.	• 500,000+ troops in Vietnam. • Sought political solution by military force in Vietnam. • Bombed North Vietnam. • Maintained N.A.T.O.	• Widened Vietnam War. • Tried to negotiate with Russia in Europe.
Nixon	Vietnamization. Detente. Nixon Doctrine. Opened China.	• Reduced U.S. Troops in Vietnam. • Maintain N.A.T.O. • Negotiate with USSR. • Diplomatic agreements with China.	• Withdrew from Vietnam. • Keep commitments in rest of world. • Use China to contain Soviet Union.

Famous Doctrines: From Monroe to Nixon

On several occasions in American history, presidents have unilaterally asserted American intentions in various parts of the world. These presidential doctrines have been made without the force of either treaty or international agreement. Yet, because they coincided with American interest in a region, they have been accepted by the American people, supported by Congress, and eventually agreed to by the international community.

The following chart outlines the four major doctrines in United States history. As you study the materials, consider under what authority America made its pronouncements about other parts of the world. Does the U.S. have the right to intervene in other nation's affairs? Also were the doctrines merely a reflection of American self-interest or did they serve international peace and order?

Famous Doctrines

	Monroe	Truman	Eisenhower	Nixon
Year	1823	1947	1957	1969
Area of World	Western Hemisphere	Greece/Turkey	Middle East	Asia
Reason for Issuance	Feared Spain would try to re-colonize. Also feared Russian action on west coast of U.S.A.	Feared Soviet moves in Greece.	Feared Soviet moves in area.	Redefine U.S. policy in world, yet reassure allies.
Principles	No new colonies in Western Hemisphere. Existing colonies left alone by U.S. U.S. would stay out of European affairs. Discourage the extension of monarchies into Americas.	U.S. would help nations resisting outside aggression.	Congress said president could assist nations resisting communist attack.	U.S. would aid friends, but not with American troops.
Example of Action	U.S. intervened Venezuela-British dispute in 1895.	$400 million to Greece and Turkey.	Troops sent to Lebanon.	Removal of American troops from Vietnam.